Contents

Any words appearing in bold, **like this**, are explained in the Glossary.

What is dinner?

Dinner is usually the last meal of the day and the biggest meal. Some people eat dinner in the late afternoon just after school, others eat later.

Many families try to sit down together for this meal. They enjoy eating good food together, and talking about the day.

What's your favourite dinner?

4

In Sri Lanka people often eat prawn curry, salad, and rice for dinner, with a drink of coconut juice.

Lots of children in the USA like chicken wraps, fruit salad, and a glass of milk for dinner.

Wiener Schnitzel is a veal cutlet. It is served with potatoes and cucumber salad. This is popular in Austria.

In Jamaica, a favourite dinner is shrimp, rice, and ochra, and a glass of carrot juice.

Why do you eat dinner?

The food you eat for dinner must supply you with **nutrients** that last until breakfast. Your body needs nutrients to grow, and for **energy** to work, play, and even to sleep.

The energy in food is measured in **kilojoules** or calories. Each food has a different amount.

How much energy is in this dinner?

110g fish (cod) cooked in 1tbsp butter	*791 kJ (189 cal)*
100g rice	*577 kJ (138 cal)*
2 wholemeal rolls and butter	*1356 kJ (324 cal)*
mixed salad and dressing	*1079 kJ (258 cal)*

tbsp = tablespoons g = grams

Using the kilojoules

Your body needs energy for everything that you do. Playing sports uses the kilojoules (kJ) from your food more quickly, but easier activities use energy, too.

This bar chart is a guide to the amount of energy a child may use during 30 minutes of these activities.

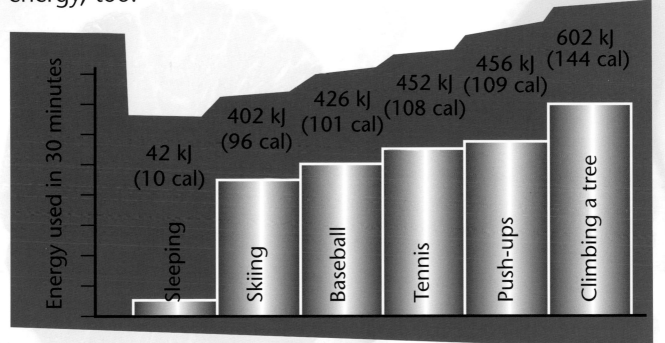

Energy used in 30 minutes

42 kJ (10 cal) — Sleeping

402 kJ (96 cal) — Skiing

426 kJ (101 cal) — Baseball

452 kJ (108 cal) — Tennis

456 kJ (109 cal) — Push-ups

602 kJ (144 cal) — Climbing a tree

Quiz

How many kilojoules would your body use if you slept for 10 hours? (Think carefully. First you need to work out how many kilojoules you would use in one hour.)

(Answer at the bottom of the page)

Answer: While sleeping for 10 hours you would use 840 kJ (200 cal).

What are the healthiest dinner foods?

Your body needs many different **nutrients** to grow and work properly. You must eat a mix of foods every day for a healthy **diet**.

The food groups needed for a healthy diet are shown in this chart.

When you understand which nutrients different foods contain, choosing good dinner foods is easier. This chart divides foods into the groups needed for good **nutrition**.

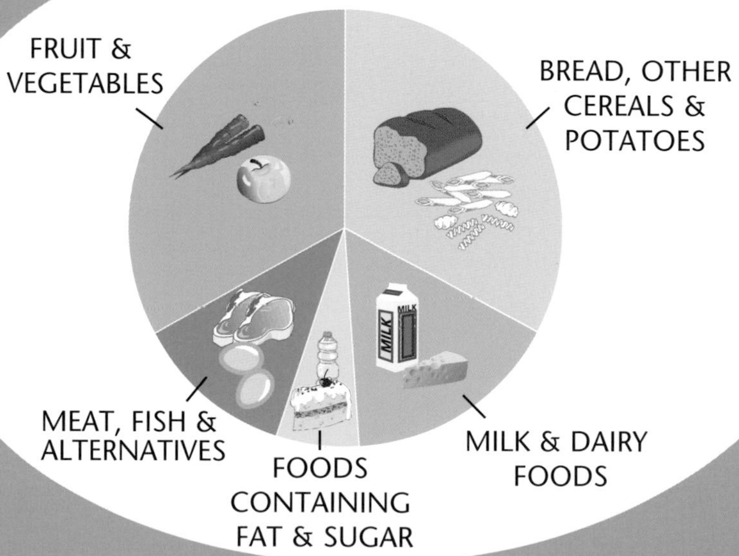

FRUIT & VEGETABLES

BREAD, OTHER CEREALS & POTATOES

MEAT, FISH & ALTERNATIVES

FOODS CONTAINING FAT & SUGAR

MILK & DAIRY FOODS

The chart above shows that some food groups should make up a smaller amount of your daily diet. If you use this chart, you can make sure that you get the food balance right.

Choosing foods from the five main food groups can help you eat a healthy dinner. Spaghetti Bolognaise contains food from the "bread, other cereals, and potatoes" group, and the "meat, fish, and alternatives" group. A salad or steamed broccoli are good vegetables for dinner. Watermelon and grapes are healthy fruits to eat. A glass of milk from the "milk and dairy foods" group completes the meal.

A healthy dinner like this contains all the fat you need.

dairy   cereals   meat   vegetables   fruit

Dinner foods and nutrition

Food contains **nutrients**, which are needed by your body for different things.

Some nutrients, like **carbohydrates**, **protein**, and **fat**, give you energy. Nutrients like **vitamins** and **minerals** keep you well and strong. Protein is also needed for growing and healing.

Which dinner foods give you these nutrients?

Carbohydrates

Fats

Proteins

10

More nutrients

Your food must also supply enough of the right vitamins and minerals to stop you getting ill.

Vitamins help your body to work properly and keep your **immune system** strong. A strong immune system stops you getting sick.

Minerals are used to grow strong bones and teeth. They also help your blood and nerves to work.

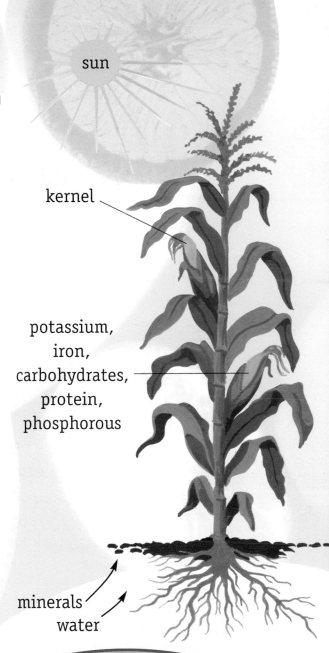

sun

kernel

potassium,
iron,
carbohydrates,
protein,
phosphorous

minerals

water

Which vitamins and minerals do you need?

You must have vitamins A, B, C, D, E, and K.

Make sure you get these minerals too—calcium, potassium, iron, magnesium, phosphorus, and zinc.

All of these are in a healthy, balanced diet.

The part of the sweetcorn plant that we eat is the kernel, also called the grain or seed. It contains the most nutrients.

11

Bread, other cereals, and potatoes for dinner

Every day you need several foods from this group. They are the best source of **carbohydrates** to give your body **energy**.

These foods also supply you with **vitamins**, **minerals**, and **fibre**. Food high in fibre helps keep your **gut** healthy.

Did you know that baby corn is a type of cereal? It's great for dipping.

Cereal grains like wheat, rice, and maize are used to make different products. Pasta, bread, and tortillas are all made from grains. Some products are made from whole grains, others are made from **refined** grains. Whole grain products are a healthy choice, as they contain more fibre and other nutrients. Refined grains have often had these nutrients removed.

Pastas are made with the flours of different grains, such as wheat or maize. The healthiest pastas are made with whole grains.

Healthy fruit and vegetables for dinner

Some of the best foods that you can eat for dinner are in the "fruit and vegetables" group. These foods have many **nutrients**, including **vitamins**, **minerals**, **carbohydrates**, and **fibre**.

Eating a mix of vegetables in a salad provides many different nutrients at once.

Dinner around the world

In Ireland, some children eat fried cabbage for dinner. The cabbage is cooked in a pan with onions, garlic, pepper, and bacon.

A healthy **diet** includes fruit and vegetables every day. You can eat several vegetables at once mixed in a salad.

Fresh, **raw** vegetables have lots of nutrients.

Broccoli salad

Always ask an adult to help you in the kitchen.

g = grams

Ask an adult to cut all of these into small pieces and place in a bowl:

1 crown of broccoli	You can add:
½ crown of cauliflower	150 g sunflower seeds
1 bunch of spring onions	250 g raisins
1 red pepper	100 g grated Cheddar cheese

Toss the ingredients together and stir in your favourite salad dressing. Refrigerate and serve.

More fruit and vegetables!

Foods in the "fruit and vegetables" group are full of good **nutrients**. Eating these foods is the best way for you to get vitamin C. This important **vitamin** gets used fast, so your body needs some every day.

Fruit and vegetables also contain other vitamins, as well as **minerals, fibre**, and **carbohydrates**.

More grapes are grown around the world than any other fruit. Some are dried to make raisins. Others are squeezed into juice.

People enjoy all kinds of fruit for dinner, such as kiwi, raisins, dates, blackberries, pears, and cranberries. If your favourite fruit is not available fresh, try to find it frozen or canned.

Frozen, canned, and fresh fruits have almost the same amount of nutrients. Canned fruits may have added sugar. Always check the food label, and look for fruits that are canned in their own juice.

All packaged foods have a label that tells you about the ingredients. These labels can help you plan a healthy diet.

Vitamins in fresh fruit

Vitamins: A, folate, & C

Vitamins: folate, & C

Vitamins: folate

Vitamins A, folate, & C

Healthy milk and dairy foods for dinner

Milk and dairy foods are rich in **nutrients**. They provide **protein**, **vitamins**, **minerals**, and **fats**.

Calcium = healthy bones

*All bones in your body are made from living **cells**. Bones need calcium every day to stay strong and healthy. Eating milk and dairy foods supplies calcium, another mineral called phosphorus, and also vitamin D. Without these nutrients, bones can get weak.*

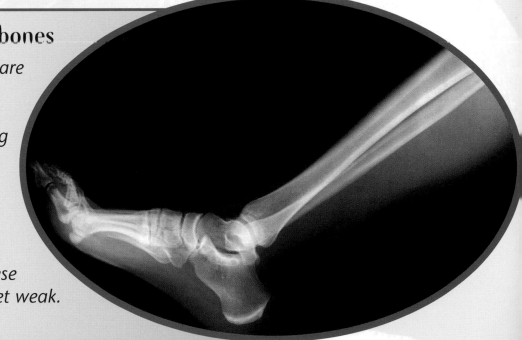

Extra ways to get calcium

Calcium is not just found in milk and dairy foods. It is also found in soya products, fish, beans, and green leafy vegetables.

x

18

Yoghurt, milk, and cheese are some of the dairy foods that you can use for your dinner menu. The healthiest choices are the ones with lower amounts of fat.

Many people enjoy frozen yoghurt for their dinner dessert.

Ice cream or yoghurt?

The diagram shows that two scoops of ice cream and two scoops of frozen yoghurt both have good nutrition, but ice cream is high in fat and kilojoules.

ICE CREAM		FROZEN YOGHURT
607 kJ (145 cal) 8 g fat	17 g carbohydrates 2-3 g protein 93-103 mg calcium	490 kJ (117 cal) 4 g fat

g = grams   mg = milligrams

Meat, fish, and alternatives for dinner

Besides meat and fish, this group includes eggs, beans, nuts, and seeds. These foods are together because they are full of **protein**. They also have **minerals** and **fats**.

It's easy to add prawns, meat, nuts, seeds, or beans to a stir fry. They are packed with protein.

The healthier dinner foods in this group are **lean** meat, fish, beans, and nuts. If you can see fat on meat, trim it off. Try to avoid eating too many fatty meat products, like sausages or burgers.

All of the beans on this page grow in pods on bushy plants. A bean is the seed of a plant. Beans are high in **fibre**, and rich in protein, **carbohydrates**, and iron. Beans are delicious in soup!

Dinner around the world

Children in Cuba sometimes eat kidney beans and rice for dinner. The beans and rice are cooked with onion, garlic, pepper, and spices.

Add spice to dinner foods

Spices and herbs are called **seasonings**. They are made from tasty parts of plants. Seasonings are used to make foods taste even better.

Cinnamon is a spice that is made from the dried bark of a cinnamon tree. The bark curls into cinnamon sticks, which can be made into powder. Cinnamon has a sweet, rich smell and taste when it is added to foods.

The bark is stripped off the cinnamon tree and dried in the sun.

Pepper, parsley, dill, and garlic are spices and herbs that are often used. All seasonings give flavour and nutrients to food. Parsley is a herb that is very rich in vitamin C.

Some sauces are mixtures of seasonings. This burger has two sauces –tomato ketchup and mustard.

Ketchup ingredients: tomatoes, tomato paste, vinegar, salt, sweetener, spices

Mustard ingredients: ground mustard seeds, vinegar, water, spices

What's for dessert?

Shortcake for dessert

Always ask an adult to help you in the kitchen.

g = grams   tbsp = tablespoons
ml = millilitres

1. Rub 200 g of wholemeal plain flour and 50 g butter together, until it looks like breadcrumbs.

2. Add:

   1 tbsp honey or 2 tbsp sugar

   1 beaten egg

   50 ml milk

   1 tbsp baking powder.

3. Beat until smooth.

4. Drop dollops of the mixture on the baking tray, to make several shortcakes.

5. Bake at 190° C/ 375° F / gas mark 5 for about 10 minutes.

6. Cool your shortcakes.

7. Serve with strawberries and whipped cream.

Dessert is a little extra food at the end of a meal, usually something sweet. Strawberry shortcake is a favourite.

Fruit gives this dessert sweetness and colour. You can use any kind of fruit instead of strawberries in this recipe.

Desserts can be healthy if you add lots of fruit to give them natural sweetness. Apple and grape juice can also be used to sweeten dishes. This means you can get the **nutrients** from the fruit, as well as a sweet taste.

Honey, juice, fruit or maple syrup are better choices than white sugar when making desserts. Sweet foods are healthier when they are natural.

Prepare a safe dinner

Germs can grow in a dirty kitchen. They can make you sick. To prepare a clean, safe dinner you will need fresh food and a clean place to work.

Wash your hands before you start, and again if you touch any raw meat or eggshells. Make sure the counter top and **cooking utensils** are clean.

Check the foods you are preparing. Most will have a date on the label. Make sure each food is fresh and safe to eat.

Mouldy food is not safe to eat. Germs are growing on it. Throw it away!

Special care

Special care is needed when you prepare meat. Hands, counter tops, and cooking utensils that touch **raw** meat must be cleaned before they touch other things.

Meats need to be well cooked to get rid of germs. Always read a cookbook for the correct temperature setting and cooking time for your meat.

Ask an adult to check that your meat is cooked and safe to eat. They may use a meat thermometer to do this.

While this 4 kg turkey cooked for 3½ hours, there was plenty of time to prepare the rest of the special dinner.

Dinner planner: lasagne

Preheat oven to 190° C/ 375° F/gas mark 5.

Always ask an adult to help you in the kitchen.

- g = grams
- **Cooking utensils:**
  - large oven proof dish
  - medium saucepan
  - large spoon
  - mixing bowl

- **Lasagne ingredients:**
  - packet of lasagne sheets
  - 750 g jar of tomato pasta sauce
  - 450 g **lean** minced beef, already cooked
  - 2 eggs
  - 250 g ricotta cheese
  - 450 g grated mozzarella cheese
  - 75 g grated Parmesan cheese

- **Other dinner ingredients:**
  - bread and butter
  - mixed salad

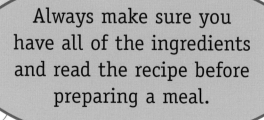

Always make sure you have all of the ingredients and read the recipe before preparing a meal.

Directions:

1. Heat the tomato sauce, 100 ml water, and the meat in the saucepan.

2. Beat the eggs and mix in the ricotta cheese and half of the Parmesan cheese.

3. Cover the bottom of the baking dish with the lasagne sheets.

4. Cover the pasta with half of the egg/ricotta mix.

5. Spread half the grated mozzarella over the egg/ricotta mix.

6. Spread a third of the tomato meat sauce over the mozzarella cheese.

7. Repeat steps 3-6.

8. Put one more layer of lasagne sheets on top.

9. Add the last third of the tomato meat sauce.

10. Top with the rest of the Parmesan cheese.

11. Cook for 30-35 minutes until it is hot and bubbly.

12. Wash and prepare the mixed salad.

13. Set the table with plates, napkins, cutlery, glasses of water, salad, salad dressing, bread, and butter.

14. Remove your lasagne from the oven and cool for 10 minutes, then cut and serve.

Lasagne is a healthy dinner that you can prepare with an adult. This meal includes foods from each of the food groups.

29

Find out for yourself

Choosing foods for a healthy diet is important, but it doesn't have to be difficult. Learn the basic food groups and how much you need from each one. Make good choices and enjoy good health.

Books to read

Look after yourself: Get Some Exercise!, Angela Royston (Heinemann Library, 2004)

Look after yourself: Eat Healthy Food!, Angela Royston (Heinemann Library, 2004)

Go Facts: Healthy Eating, Paul McEvoy (A & C Black, 2005)

Healthy Body Cookbook: Fun Activities and Delicious Recipes for Kids, Joan D'Amico and Karen Eich Drummond (John Wiley & Sons, 1998)

Using the Internet

Explore the Internet to find out more about healthy dinner foods. Websites can change so if some of the links below no longer work, don't worry. Use a search engine, such as **www.yahooligans.com** or **www.internet4kids.com** and type in key words such as "dinner foods," "healthy diet" or "dinner nutrition."

Websites

www.nutrition.org.uk Click on "Education", then "Cook club" for some great recipe ideas.

www.eatwell.gov.uk There is lots of information about diet and health here, as well as quizzes and games.

www.5aday.nhs.uk Find out easy ways to get your 5-a-day, and some delicious smoothie recipes.

Glossary

carbohydrate the nutrient in food that gives you energy

cell the body's smallest building block of living tissue

cooking utensils the knives, spatulas, and small tools used to prepare food

diet what you usually eat and drink

energy the power needed for your body to work and stay alive

fats nutrient from food that gives you energy

fibre material in foods that is not digested but helps carry the food through the digestive system

germ a tiny living creature that can cause disease

immune system the part of your body that protects you from disease and infection

kilojoule a measurement of food energy

lean meat that has very little fat

mineral a type of nutrient needed to make the body work correctly

nutrient substance (such as vitamin, mineral, or protein) that people need to grow and stay healthy

nutrition the part of food that your body can use

protein nutrient in food that gives you energy and is used for growth and repair

raw food that is raw has not been cooked, processed, or refined

refined purified or processed by removing parts of the plant

seasoning a herb or spice added to food to give it more flavour

vitamin a type of nutrient in food that the body needs to stay healthy and work correctly

whole grains grains, such as oats, wheat, corn, or rice, that have all or most of their natural fibre and nutrients

Index